HISTORIC BUILDINGS OF BOSTON

A Coloring Book of Architecture

by Scott Clowney

Commonwealth Editions

Carlisle, Massachusetts

Dedication

To Lucy, Desi, and Mr. T—my traveling companions—who make sightseeing such a rewarding experience.

Acknowledgments

To the city of Boston, thank you for your hospitality. You now have a special place in my heart. Special thanks to the team at Applewood Books.

978-1-64194-001-6

Text edits by Applewood Books.

The display type is Petit Four, created by David Kerkhoff in 2015.

Published by Commonwealth Editions, an imprint of Applewood Books, Inc., P.O. Box 27, Carlisle, Massachusetts 01741

Visit us on the web at www.commonwealtheditions.com
Visit Scott Clowney on the web at www.scottclowney.com

INTRODUCTION

I visited Boston for the first time in 2017 and had a great experience!

After an early check-in at the hotel, we set our sights on the North End and downtown neighborhoods. I eagerly anticipated beginning our tour where Boston's oldest buildings reside.

The Old State House, considered the oldest public building in Boston, is beautifully preserved—a true highlight on the Freedom Trail during our first day of sightseeing. Wonderfully juxtaposed against newer, taller buildings, it serves as a window to the past.

Day two of the tour took us to Mission Hill, Fenway/Kenmore, and Back Bay. We had a lot of buildings to see and a lot of streets to walk.

Not far from the Boston Latin School, after museum hopping in the morning, we made our way to Fenway Park, the oldest ballpark in Major League Baseball. Go Sox! Later, we discovered the Berkeley Building, an elegant Beaux-Arts commercial structure on the corner of Berkeley and Boylston Streets. The building's ornamental terra-cotta, metal-framed glass bays, and crowning balustrade proudly reflect a bygone era in this busy commercial district.

We spent our last day exploring Charlestown and meandering through Beacon Hill. On our journey across the Charlestown Bridge toward the U.S.S. *Constitution*, we looked out at the soaring Leonard P. Zakim Bunker Hill Memorial Bridge, part of the city's "Big Dig" project. It's a visual masterpiece, a cable-stayed bridge that is not only functional but also attractive. At the Bunker Hill Monument, we climbed 294 steps for majestic city views. Between Charlestown and Beacon Hill, we secured tickets for an architectural boat tour that was packed with points of interest, a great way to see the city from a different point of view. Beacon Hill was beautiful, a neighborhood with charming details: brick sidewalks, cobblestone streets, gas lamps, shuttered windows, and flowering window boxes.

Boston greeted us with open arms. We fell in love with the city's diverse neighborhoods, eclectic food scene, waterfront presence, and walkability. The symbiotic relationship between historic and contemporary structures impressed us. Each encounter felt like a discovery worth a thousand words—Boston delivered and we shall return!

—Scott Clowney

CONTENTS

OLD NORTH CHURCH

LOCATION: **193 Salem Street**

NEIGHBORHOOD: **North End**

ARCHITECTS: **William Price; Charles Bulfinch
(1807 steeple)**

A National Historic Landmark, Old North Church is the oldest standing church in Boston, built in 1723. It marks the site of lanterns that were displayed in the steeple to send a warning to Charlestown patriots across the Charles River about the movements of the British army en route to Lexington and Concord. In the 1860 poem "Paul Revere's Ride," Henry Wadsworth Longfellow coined the phrase "One if by land, and two if by sea" to illustrate the reconnaissance of this historic event.

CLOUGH HOUSE

LOCATION: **21 Unity Street**

NEIGHBORHOOD: **North End**

BUILDER: **Ebenezer Clough**

Circa 1715, this house was built by Ebenezer Clough, a master bricklayer, for his home. It is a rare surviving example of a brick row house in the city and was converted into apartments in 1806 after the family moved out. Today the building is owned by the Old North Church Association. Captain Jackson's Historic Chocolate Shop, which explores the history of chocolate and how it was both produced and consumed in the eighteenth century, occupies the building, along with the printing office of Edes & Gill, where visitors can see an eighteenth-century printing press and experience the colonial-era printing process.

PAUL REVERE HOUSE

LOCATION: **19 North Square**

NEIGHBORHOOD: **North End**

ARCHITECTS: **John Jeffs; Joseph Chandler (1907 restoration)**

This was the Elizabethan Tudor–style home of American patriot Paul Revere, who remains famous for his ride to warn Lexington of oncoming British troops. It is downtown Boston's oldest building, built in 1680 for Robert Howard, a wealthy merchant. Revere owned this home from 1770 to 1800; thereafter, it became a sailor's boardinghouse, immigrant tenement, and shops. The house opened as a historic house museum in 1908, making it one of the oldest house museums in America.

EBENEZER HANCOCK HOUSE

LOCATION: **10 Marshall Street**

NEIGHBORHOOD: **Downtown**

BUILDER: **John Hancock**

Considered the oldest brick building in Boston, this eighteenth-century three-story masonry building with residence and shop was completed in 1767 for Ebenezer, the younger brother of John. As deputy paymaster general of the Continental army, he dispersed money to troops during the Revolutionary War. Later the building became the residence and business of a china and glass merchant. A shoe merchant occupied the building from 1798 to 1963, one of the longest continuously operating shoe stores in the country. It was renovated in the 1970s for the law firm of Swartz & Swartz, P.C., and today is classified as a National Historic Landmark.

BOSTON CITY HALL

LOCATION: 1 City Hall Square

NEIGHBORHOOD: Downtown

ARCHITECTS: Kallmann McKinnell & Knowles; Campbell, Aldrich & Nulty; and LeMessurier Associates

The design for Boston City Hall was the winning entry in an international design competition in 1962. Completed in 1968, the building marks the seat of city government, with offices for the mayor and city council. Though celebrated in the 1960s and 1970s for its progressive design, today the building remains controversial due in part to its visual characteristics but also to the large desolate plaza which the building overlooks. The building is deeply Brutalist in style, constructed of precast and poured-in-place concrete with rigid cantilevered concrete forms that seemingly alienate it from nearby buildings.

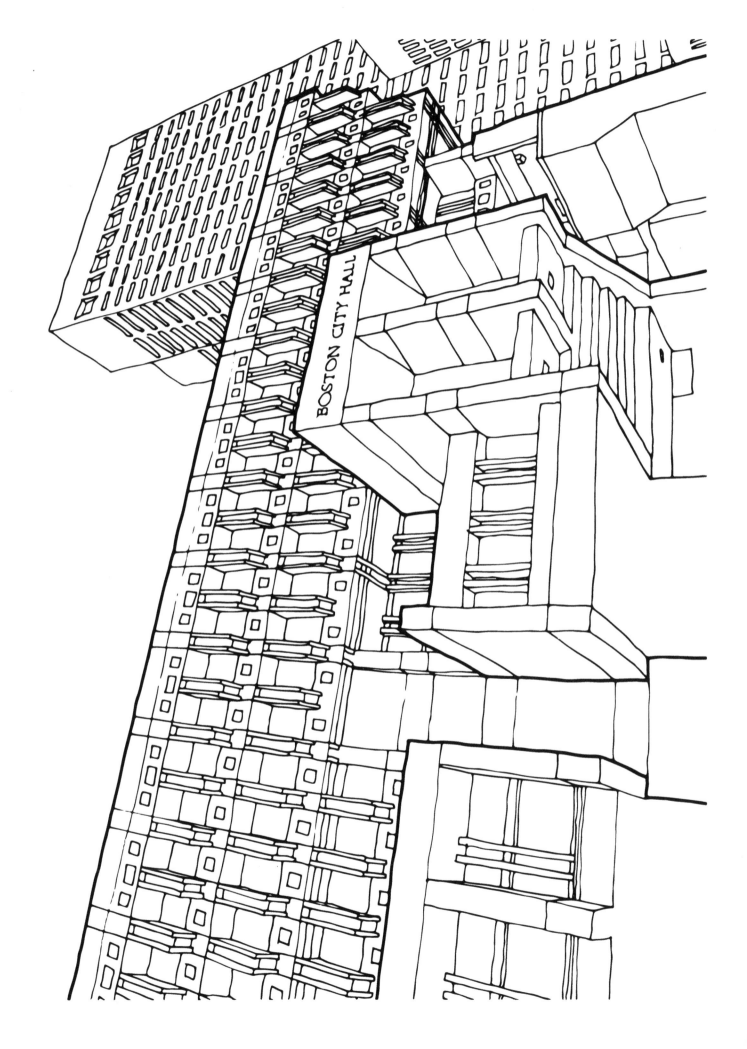

FANEUIL HALL MARKETPLACE

LOCATION: 4 South Market Street

NEIGHBORHOOD: Downtown

ARCHITECTS: John Smybert; Charles Bulfinch (1806 renovations and additions); Benjamin Thompson (1970 renovations)

SCULPTOR: Anne Whitney

Built in 1742 in the style of an English country market, this building was—and remains—the site of political activities and speeches. Samuel Adams and George Washington presided over activities here, and colonists famously established the doctrine of "no taxation without representation." Expanded in 1826 to include nearby Quincy Market, the entire area was preserved in the 1970s after years of decay and neglect. Shops and restaurants attract local patrons and tourists, as do outdoor entertainers including jugglers, magicians, and musicians. A nineteenth-century sculpture of Samuel Adams by Anne Whitney adorns the west plaza opposite Boston City Hall.

QUINCY MARKET

LOCATION: 4 South Market Street

NEIGHBORHOOD: Downtown

ARCHITECT: Alexander Parris

Completed in 1826, this Greek Revival–style structure is named in honor of Josiah Quincy, who served as mayor of Boston from 1823 to 1828. Part of Faneuil Hall Marketplace, the building is flanked by North Market and South Market, each built in response to overcrowding at Quincy and Faneuil Hall. Produce, meat, and dairy goods were sold here. In the 1970s, the buildings were transformed into a festival marketplace with eateries, specialty shops, and offices.

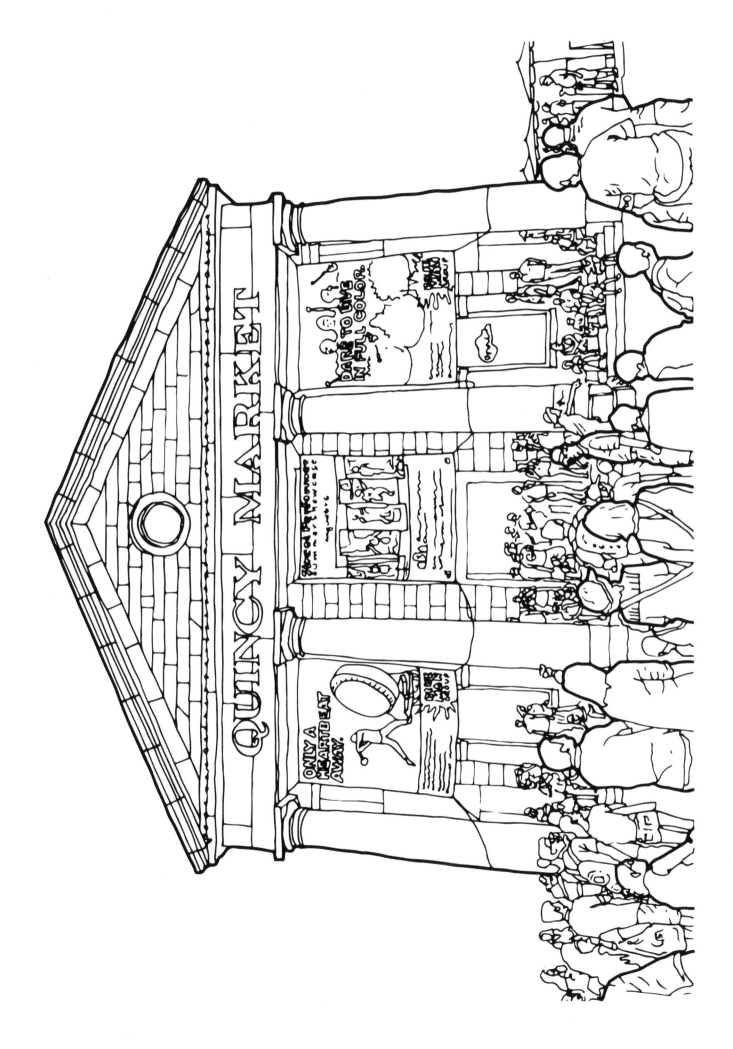

CUSTOM HOUSE TOWER

LOCATION: 3 McKinley Square

NEIGHBORHOOD: Downtown

**ARCHITECTS: Ammi Burnham Young (1849);
Peabody & Stearns (1913–15 tower addition)**

The result of a winning competition entry in 1837, this building was completed in 1849 with a neoclassical design consisting of Greek and Roman characteristics, including Doric columns, a portico, and a dome. The building was located on land that was filled in, once part of the city's waterfront edge. The 496-foot tower, added in 1915 by Peabody & Stearns, remained the tallest structure in Boston until 1964, when the Prudential Tower was built. The tower contains a 22-foot-diameter marble-and-bronze clock on each of its sides. An observation deck on the twenty-sixth floor offers expansive views of downtown Boston and the harbor. Today, the Marriott Custom House Hotel occupies the building.

GRAIN EXCHANGE BUILDING

LOCATION: **177 Milk Street**

NEIGHBORHOOD: **Downtown**

ARCHITECT: **Shepley, Rutan and Coolidge**

Located near the Custom House Tower, this elegant building was completed in 1892 in a Romanesque Revival style associated with renowned architect H. H. Richardson. Originally occupied by the Boston Chamber of Commerce until 1902, it later became the Flour and Grain Exchange. The triangular footprint is unique and the result of site conditions. The northwest corner of the structure is rounded with a conical roof and peaked dormers. It was restored in 1988 and has been occupied by many tenants in the twenty-first century.

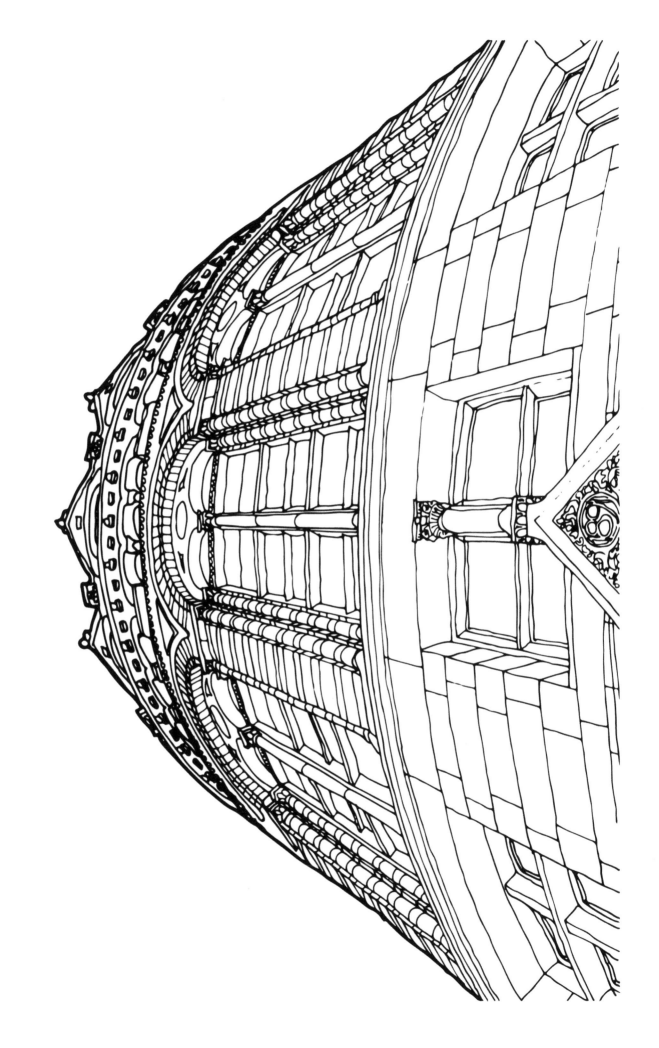

SOUTH STATION

LOCATION: **700 Atlantic Avenue**

NEIGHBORHOOD: **Downtown**

ARCHITECT: **Shepley, Rutan and Coolidge**

When it was completed in 1898, South Station was the largest train terminal in the world and Boston's largest structure. Service commenced on New Year's Day in 1899. Considered the busiest train station in the world, it handled 38 million passengers a year by 1913. The clock, manufactured by the E. Howard Watch & Clock Company of nearby Roxbury, stands as the only remaining double, three-legged escapement mechanism in New England. Today, it's part of the Michael S. Dukakis South Station Transportation Center, Boston's busiest transit hub.

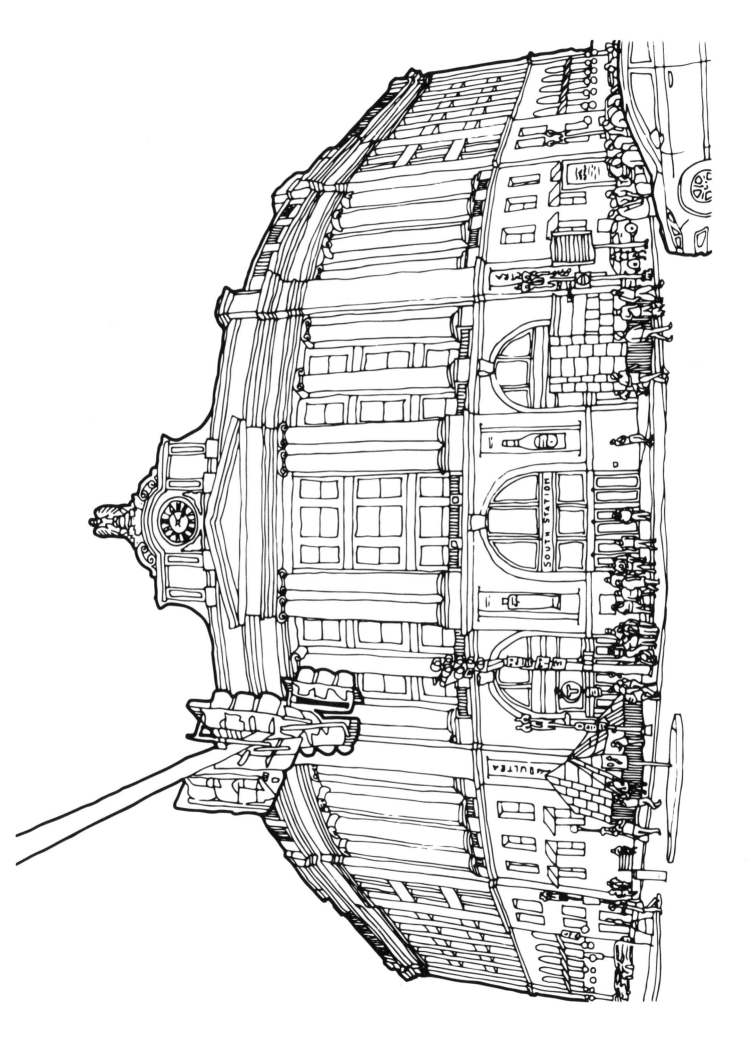

OLD STATE HOUSE

LOCATION: **206 Washington Street**

NEIGHBORHOOD: **Downtown**

ARCHITECTS: **Original architect unknown; rebuilt 1748; Isaiah Rogers (1830 alterations); George Albert Clough (1881–82 restoration); Goody, Clancy & Associates (1991 renovations)**

Completed in 1713, the Old State House was built to house the government offices of the Massachusetts Bay Colony. It is the oldest surviving public building in Boston. In what came to be known as the Boston Massacre, British soldiers fired upon a crowd of colonists in front of this building in 1770, killing five and wounding others. The Declaration of Independence was first announced from the balcony overlooking the town square. In 2014, the building was extensively repaired and today it operates as a museum.

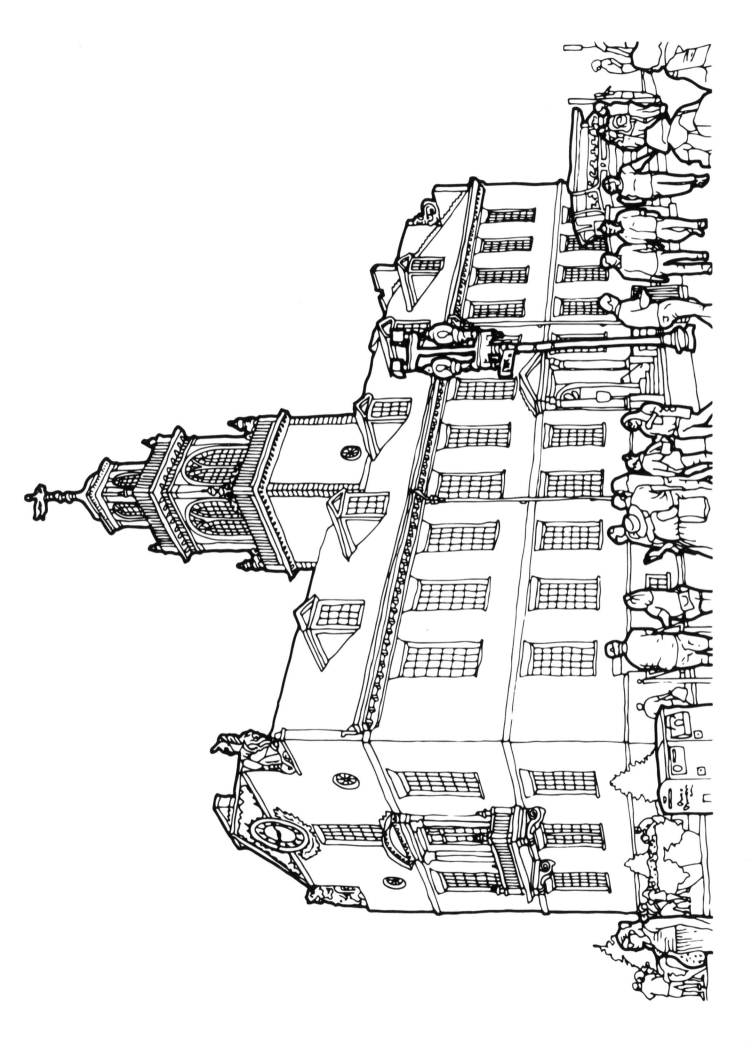

OLD SOUTH MEETING HOUSE

LOCATION: **310 Washington Street**

NEIGHBORHOOD: **Downtown**

ARCHITECT: **Robert Twelves**

At the time of its completion in 1729, Old South Meeting House was the largest building in colonial Boston and used for worship by the Puritans who founded the Massachusetts Bay Colony. As tensions grew between the American colonies and Britain, the site became a gathering place for colonists to protest British rule and taxation. In December 1773, events here led to the Boston Tea Party, where Samuel Adams directed the Sons of Liberty to destroy more than 300 crates of tea from the East India Trading Company. The British later occupied the building in 1775 and destroyed the interior. In 1872, it was almost destroyed in the Great Fire of Boston, and it came close to demolition again in 1876 before preservation was finally secured. The building opened as a museum in 1877.

OLD CITY HALL

LOCATION: **45 School Street**

NEIGHBORHOOD: **Downtown**

ARCHITECTS: **Gridley J. F. Bryant and Arthur D. Gilman; Finegold Alexander Architects (1970s adaptive reuse)**

The Boston Latin School, attended by such notable figures as Benjamin Franklin, John Hancock, and Samuel Adams, originally occupied this site from 1704 to 1748. It was the city's first public school and the oldest educational institution in the country. Later, renowned architect Charles Bulfinch designed the Suffolk County Courthouse on this site. In 1841, it was repurposed as City Hall and rebuilt 1865 in the French Second Empire style, an architectural design originating in France during the reign of Napoleon III from 1852 to 1870. When the current City Hall was built, the building was renovated into restaurant and office space.

ISABELLA STEWART GARDNER MUSEUM

LOCATION: 25 Evans Way

NEIGHBORHOOD: Fenway-Kenmore

ARCHITECTS: Willard T. Sears;
Renzo Piano (2012 addition)

Inspired by the Palazzo Barbaro in Venice, Italy, Isabella Gardner commissioned architect Willard Sears to design a Venetian-style home on the Fenway that would serve as a large museum for her extensive art collection. Originally called Fenway Court, the elaborate building was completed in 1901 and opened to guests just two years later. In its large flower-filled interior courtyard and numerous exhibition rooms, Gardner wanted an intimate setting for the art, which was unlike most museums of the time. Her collection includes works by Michelangelo, Degas, and Whistler, among others. The entire collection, including the museum, remains in place as she requested in her will. In 1990, the museum became famous for a theft of thirteen works, which have never been recovered.

BOSTON LATIN SCHOOL

LOCATION: 78 Avenue Louis Pasteur

NEIGHBORHOOD: Fenway-Kenmore

**ARCHITECTS: Original architect unknown;
HMFH Architects (2001 renovations and addition)**

The oldest public school in America, founded in 1635 to prepare students for college, this building, which opened in 1922, marks the fifth site of the school. The first site is now marked by Old City Hall, where a statue of Benjamin Franklin stands. Franklin, along with John Hancock, Samuel Adams, and two additional signers of the Declaration of Independence, attended the Boston Latin School. Since 1972 the school has been coeducational.

MUSEUM OF FINE ARTS, BOSTON

LOCATION: **465 Huntington Avenue**

NEIGHBORHOOD: **Fenway-Kenmore**

ARCHITECT: **Guy Lowell (1907–1909); Foster + Partners with Childs Bertman Tseckares Inc. (2010 addition)**

The Museum of Fine Arts once overlooked Copley Square near the Boston Public Library and Trinity Church. In 1909, the museum opened at its current location on Huntington Avenue. Noted artist John Singer Sargent is attributed with the rotunda and colonnade frescoes inside the building. Today, it's one of the largest museums in the world, with nearly 500,000 works of art in its collection. In 2010, the museum expanded with a four-story, fifty-three-gallery addition known as the Art of the Americas Wing. *Appeal to the Great Spirit*, a bronze statue by sculptor Cyrus Dallin, stands outside the museum's Huntington Avenue entrance.

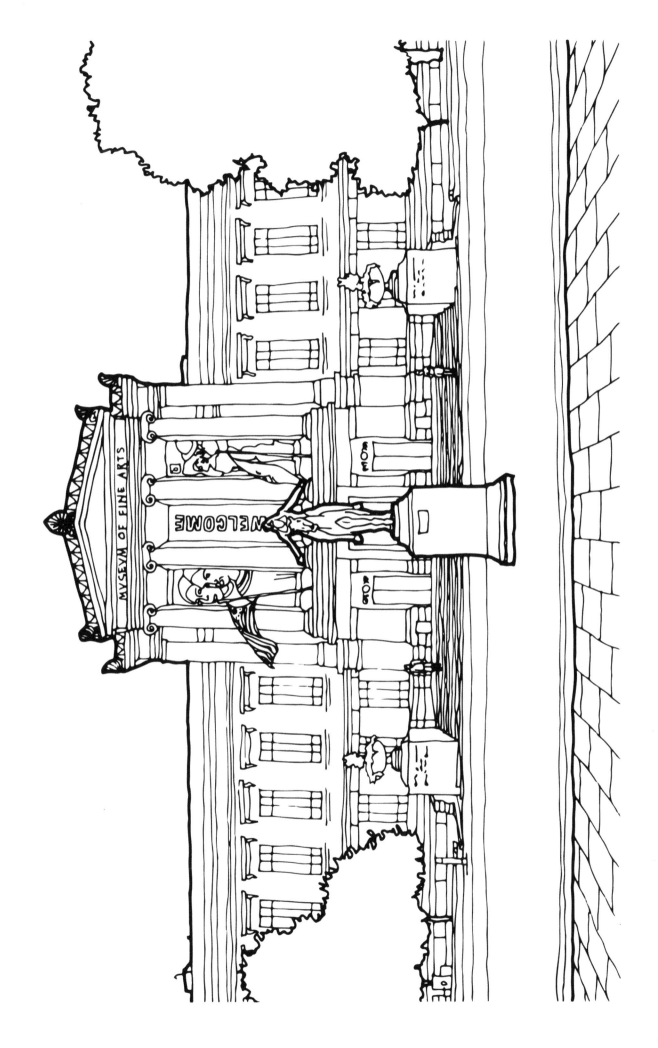

CHURCH OF CHRIST, SCIENTIST ("MOTHER CHURCH")

LOCATION: 210 Massachusetts Avenue

NEIGHBORHOOD: Back Bay

ARCHITECTS: Franklin I. Welch (1894 original Mother Church); Charles Brigham (1904–06 Mother Church extension); S. S. Beman (1904–06)

Established by Mary Baker Eddy, founder of Christian Science, the original building was completed 1894 in a Romanesque style. The large extension, which includes the dome, was completed in 1906 in a Byzantine-Renaissance style. At 224 feet, the height of the dome is 81 feet shorter than the Statue of Liberty. This church contains one of the world's largest pipe organs. The building is currently undergoing renovations.

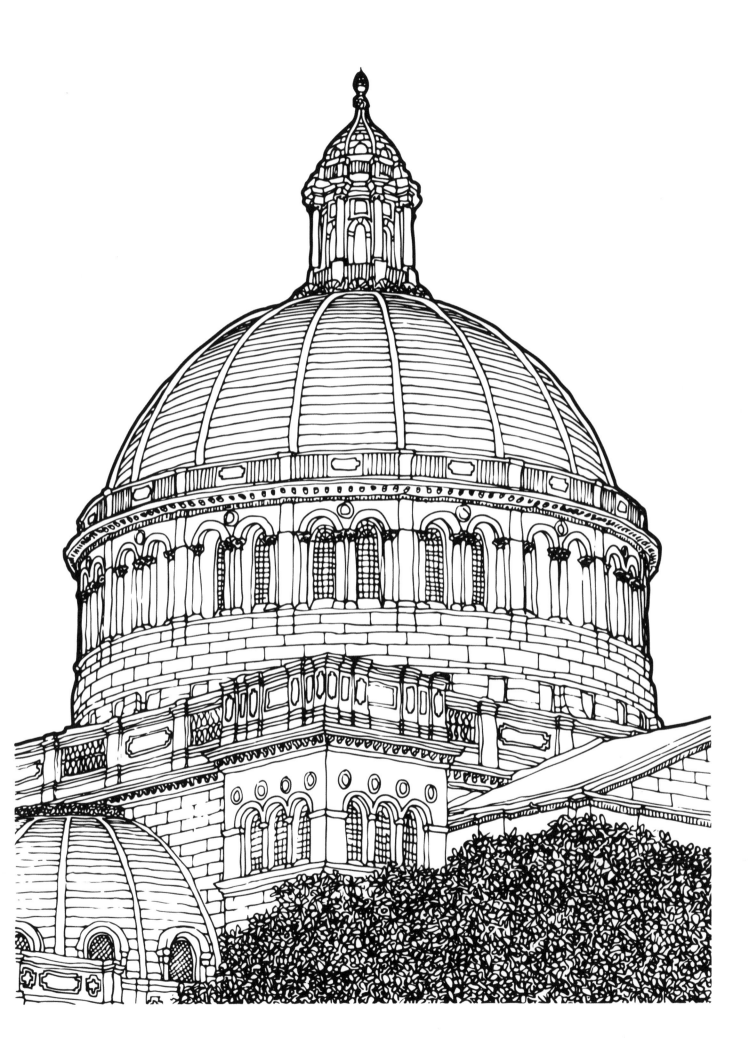

HORTICULTURAL HALL, MASSACHUSETTS HORTICULTURAL SOCIETY

LOCATION: **300 Massachusetts Avenue**

NEIGHBORHOOD: **Fenway-Kenmore**

ARCHITECT: **Wheelwright & Haven**

Completed in 1901 as the third building for the Massachusetts Horticultural Society, it became home to many horticultural organizations. The Beaux-Arts–style building contains a 300-seat lecture hall and exhibition space. Today, the building is owned by the Christian Science Church, with plans for restoration and renovation. The horticultural society is currently located at Elm Bank Horticulture Center in Dover, Massachusetts.

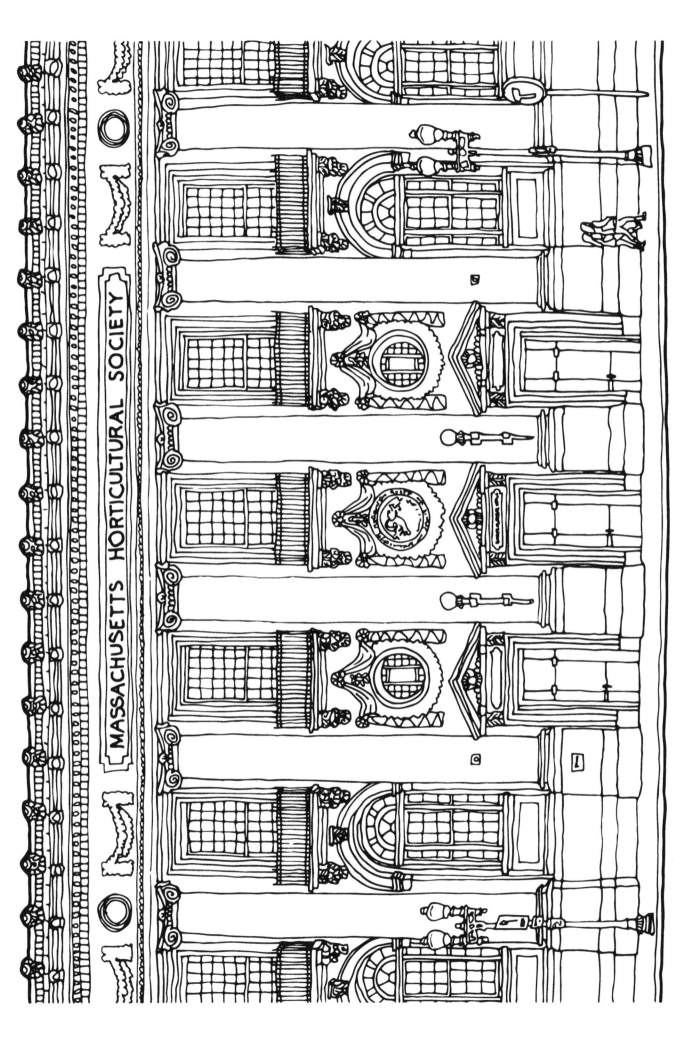

SYMPHONY HALL

LOCATION: 301 Massachusetts Avenue
NEIGHBORHOOD: Fenway-Kenmore
ARCHITECT: McKim, Mead & White

Symphony Hall opened in 1900, built for the Boston Symphony Orchestra, which now presents over 250 concerts a year. Acoustical consultant Wallace Clement Sabine contributed to the design of the concert hall, which was the first to employ scientifically derived acoustical principles. The rectangular or "shoebox" shape with angled stage walls helps direct sound to the audience. It is considered one of the best-sounding classical concert venues in the world.

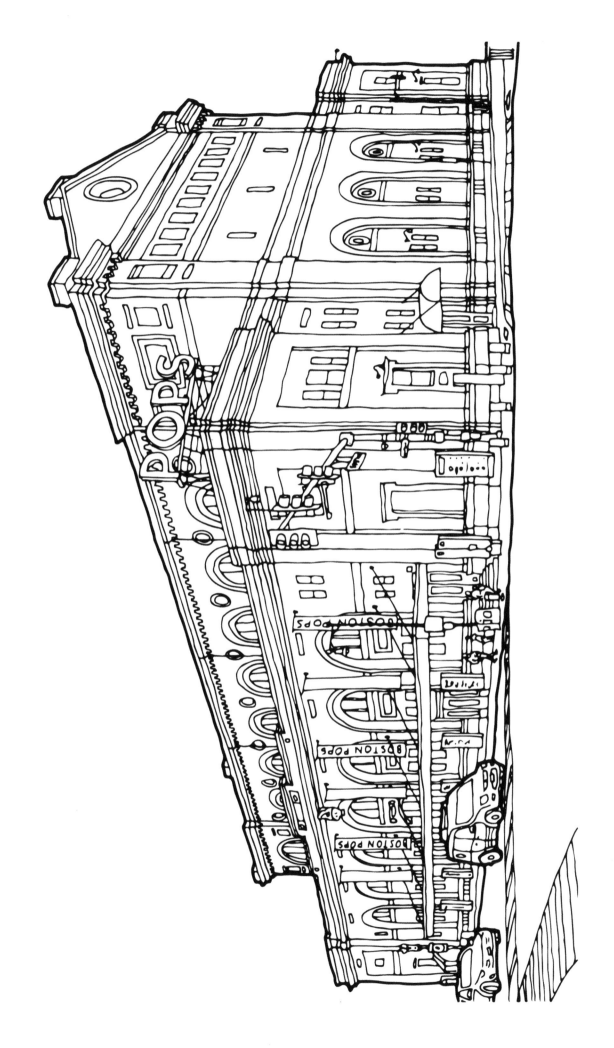

FENWAY PARK

LOCATION: **4 Jersey Street Extension**

NEIGHBORHOOD: **Fenway-Kenmore**

ARCHITECT: **James McLaughlin**

Fenway Park opened as home to the Boston Red Sox days after the sinking of the R.M.S. *Titanic* in April 1912. It is the oldest ballpark in Major League Baseball. Boston beat the New York Yankees during the first game. Babe Ruth, who gained fame with the Yankees, began his career with the Red Sox. Just over thirty-seven feet high, the "Green Monster" is a large left field green wall popularized at the ballpark as a target for right-handed hitters. The official mascot, Wally the Green Monster, is named after the wall. Over the years, Fenway Park has been renovated and expanded several times. The ballpark is listed on the National Register of Historic Places.

BURRAGE MANSION

LOCATION: 314 Commonwealth Avenue

NEIGHBORHOOD: Back Bay

ARCHITECT: Charles Brigham

Built 1899 by L. D. Willcutt & Son builders, the design for this luxurious home was inspired by Chenonceaux, the Loire Valley chateau celebrated for its lavish materials, craftsmanship, and intricate architectural details. It was a winter home for original owners Albert and Alice Burrage. Albert was an attorney, businessman, and philanthropist, as well as president of several gas lighting companies, owner of several chemical companies, and organizer of the Amalgamated Copper Company. After 1947, when Alice died, the property changed ownership and became medical offices and later a nursing home and elder-care facility. In the early 2000s, the building became Burrage Mansion Condominium, with four units, one of them occupied for a time by Tom Brady, football quarterback for the New England Patriots.

PRUDENTIAL TOWER

LOCATION: **800 Boylston Street**

NEIGHBORHOOD: **Back Bay**

ARCHITECT: **Charles Luckman Associates**

Completed in 1964 and built for the Prudential Insurance Company of America, this is Boston's second tallest building at 749 feet. It was the tallest building in North America outside of New York when it was completed. This modern skyscraper is located on grounds formerly made of marsh and train tracks for the Boston and Albany Railroad. The glass curtain wall contains over 8,200 windows. The Skywalk Observatory on the fiftieth floor offers 360-degree views of the city. The building is currently owned by Boston Properties.

KINGSLEY MONTESSORI SCHOOL

LOCATION: **26 Exeter Street (181 Newbury Street)**

NEIGHBORHOOD: **Back Bay**

ARCHITECTS: **Henry Walker Hartwell and William Cummings Richardson of Hartwell and Richardson; Clarence H. Blackall (1914 renovation)**

This 23,000-square-foot Richardsonian Romanesque building was built in 1884 for the First Spiritual Temple, owned by the Working Union of Progressive Spiritualists, which later became known as the Spiritual Fraternity. From 1914 to 1984, the building was home to the Exeter Street Theatre, a motion picture theater. In 2005, it became home to the Kingsley Montessori School.

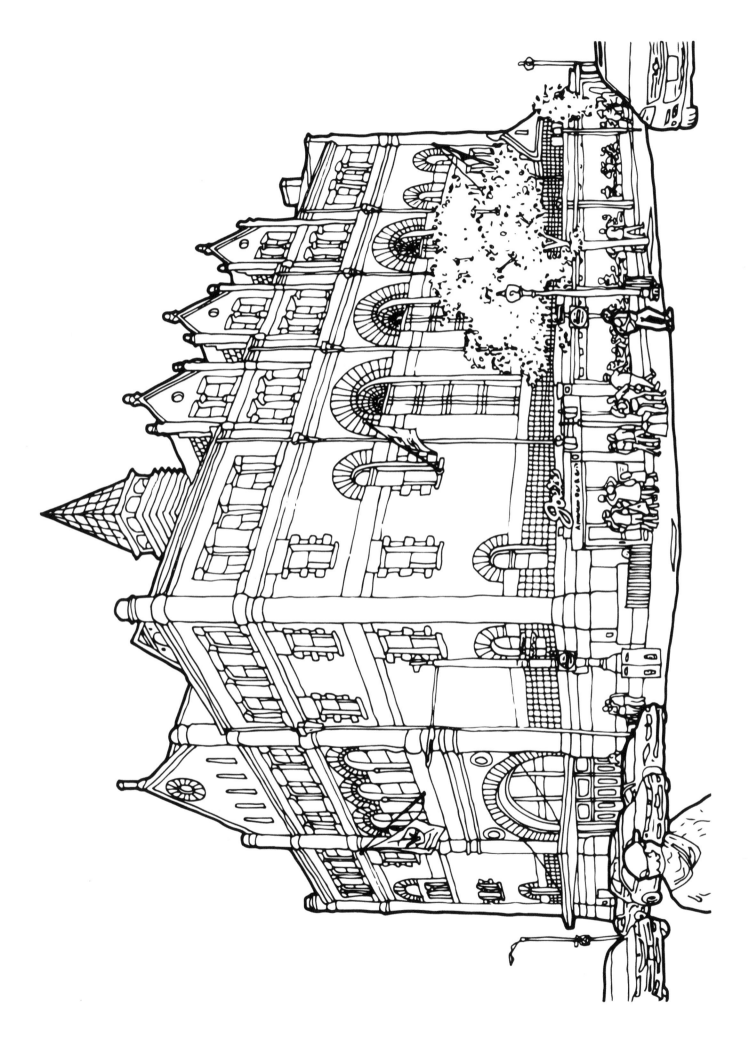

BOSTON PUBLIC LIBRARY, McKIM BUILDING

LOCATION: **700 Boylston Street**

NEIGHBORHOOD: **Back Bay**

ARCHITECT: **Charles Follen McKim
of McKim, Mead & White**

SCULPTOR: **Bela Lyon Pratt**

Built 1895 in the Renaissance Revival style, the library is located at Copley Square opposite Trinity Church. The collection holds over 1.2 million books and documents. Outside, bronze statues by sculptor Bela Lyon Pratt, who was mentored by Augustus Saint-Gaudens, rest on granite bases at the entrance to the historic McKim Building. They signify allegorical female figures, one representing "Art" with a palette and paintbrush, the other representing "Science" with a sphere. The statues were installed in 1912.

JOHN HANCOCK TOWER

LOCATION: **200 Clarendon Street**

NEIGHBORHOOD: **Back Bay**

ARCHITECT: **Henry N. Cobb of I. M. Pei & Partners**

This sixty-story, 790-foot-high modern glass skyscraper was built in 1976 for the John Hancock Mutual Life Insurance Company. Though the building was plagued by engineering problems during and after construction, such as warped retaining walls and falling glass windowpanes, it received the Twenty-five Year Award in 2011 from the American Institute of Architects because of its architectural significance and longevity. Not only is it the tallest building in Boston, it is the tallest building in New England. Today the building is owned by Boston Properties and is called 200 Clarendon.

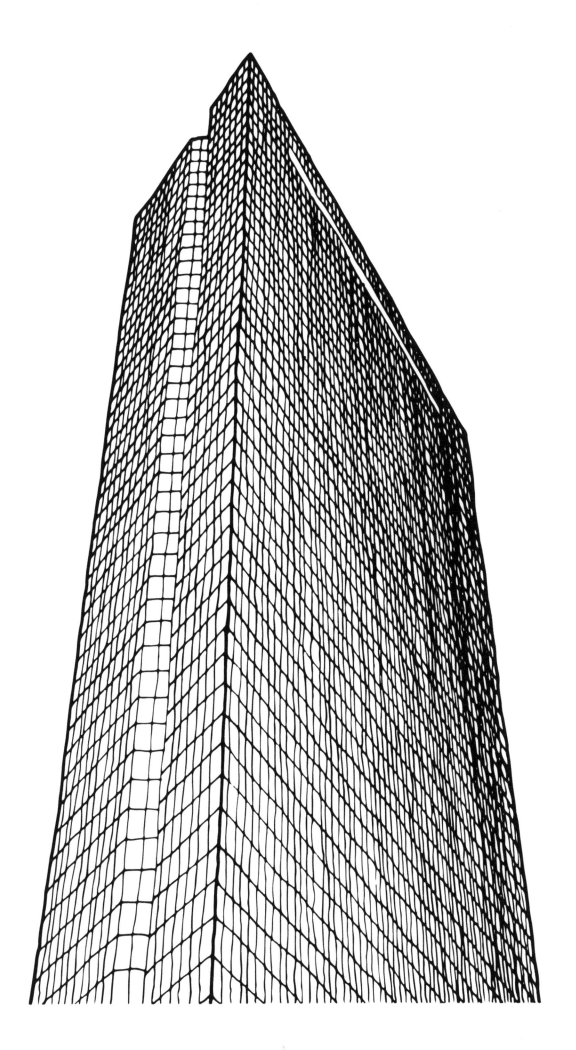

BERKELEY BUILDING

LOCATION: **414–426 Boylston Street**

NEIGHBORHOOD: **Back Bay**

ARCHITECTS: **Stephen R. H. Codman and Constant-Desire Despradelle**

Built in 1905, this Beaux-Arts–style, six-story commercial building contains ground level retail and upper level office space. Located at the intersection of Berkeley and Boylston Streets, the building was constructed with a steel frame structure and reinforced concrete. The exterior is visually significant, clad in white terra-cotta by the Atlantic Terra Cotta Company of New York City. Popular from the 1890s to the 1930s for its durable, fireproof, and aesthetically pleasing qualities, the terra-cotta here was created with playful sea motifs such as fish, sea serpents, seashells, and seaweed.

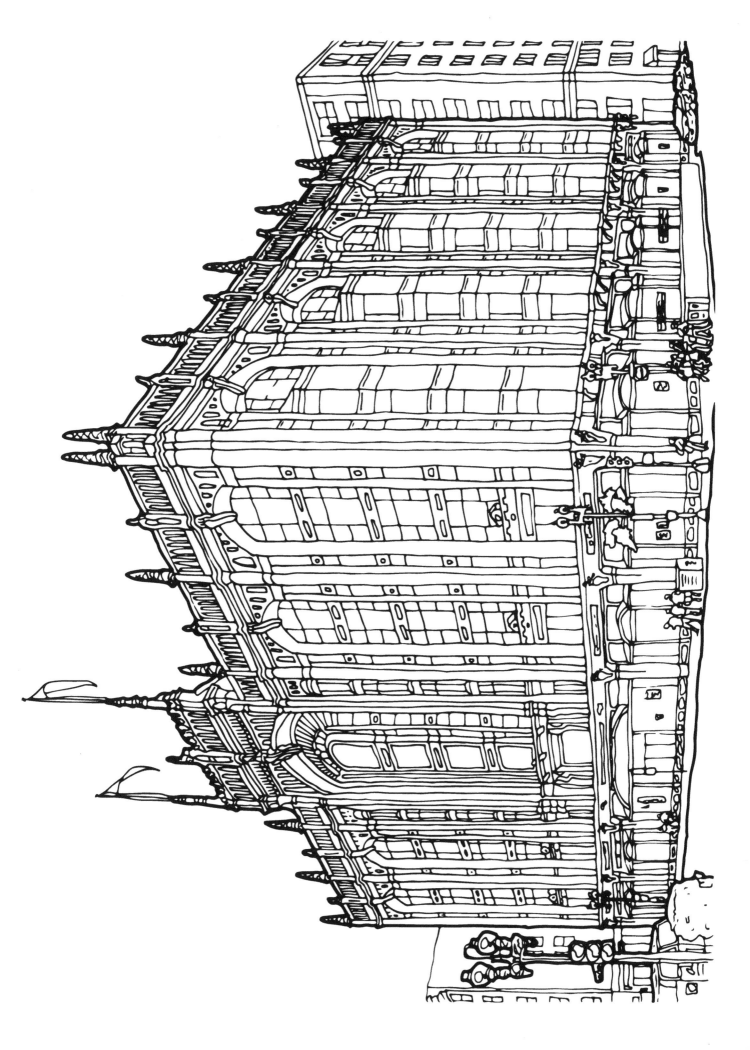

BOSTON PUBLIC GARDEN

LOCATION: Between Arlington Street & Charles Street and between Beacon Street & Boylston Street

NEIGHBORHOOD: Back Bay

LANDSCAPE ARCHITECT: Frederick Law Olmsted

Established in 1837 as the first public botanical garden in America, the park was designed in the English landscape garden style by renowned landscape architect Frederick Law Olmsted. It is located on land once comprised of mudflats, which were filled in using earth from Mount Vernon, the tip of Beacon Hill. The park contains pathways, a bridge, a pond, and formal plantings cared for by the city. Native and nonnative trees were planted throughout the park. The famous swan boats began operating in 1877 and remain a popular attraction to this day. A bench in the park is dedicated to actor Robin Williams, who starred in the film *Good Will Hunting*, which was set in Boston.

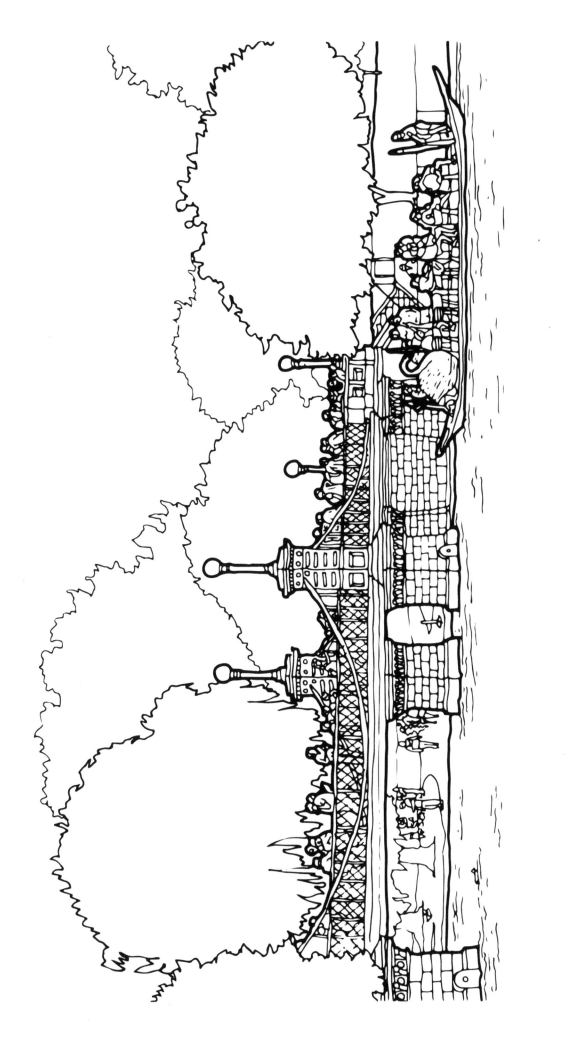

U.S.S. CONSTITUTION MUSEUM

LOCATION: **Building 22, Charlestown Navy Yard**

NEIGHBORHOOD: **Charlestown**

ARCHITECT: **Alexander Parris; James H. Ballou (museum)**

The original building was completed in 1833, designed by Alexander Parris, architect of Quincy Market in downtown Boston. Known as Building 22 (the Engine House), it was an old pump house for Dry Dock #1, the Charlestown Navy Yard's first naval dry dock. It housed the steam engines, boiler room, pumps, and wells for the discharging of water from the dock. The building was made of fireproof brick and faced with granite quarried in Quincy, Massachusetts. The museum is dedicated to the collection, preservation, and interpretation of stories relevant to "Old Ironsides," otherwise known as the U.S.S. *Constitution*, the oldest commissioned warship afloat in the world. Designed by James H. Ballou, the museum opened to the public in 1976.

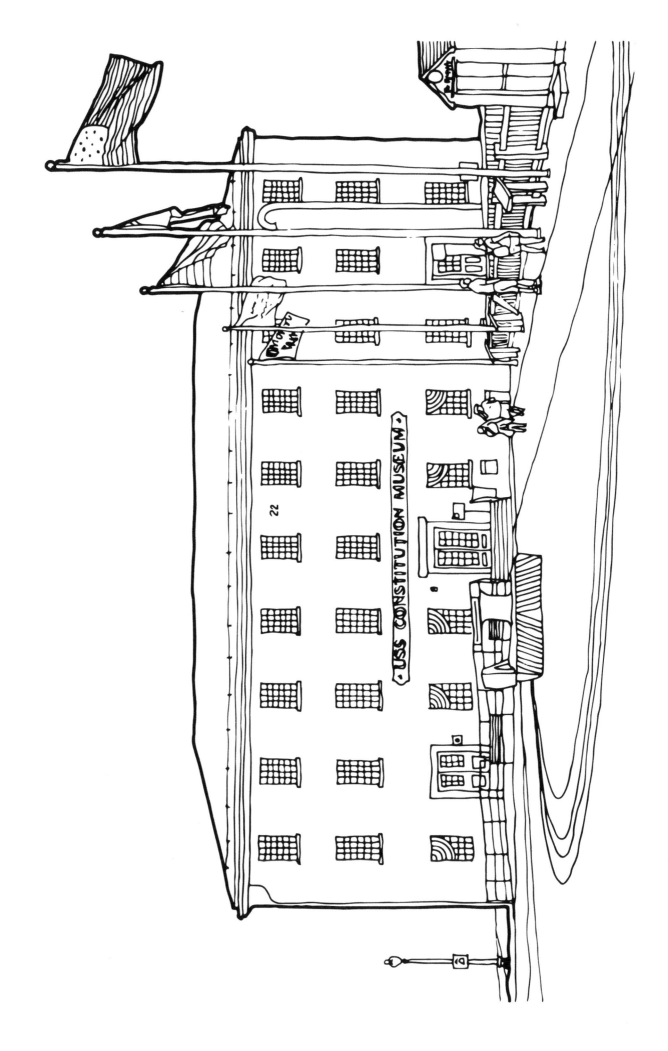

BUNKER HILL MONUMENT

LOCATION: Monument Square

NEIGHBORHOOD: Charlestown

ARCHITECT: Solomon Willard

Completed in 1842, this granite obelisk is like the Washington Monument in Washington, D.C., but less than half the height. Established by the Bunker Hill Monument Association, the tower was halted twice in construction because of a lack of funds. The 221-foot-tall monument contains 294 steps. It commemorates the Battle of Bunker Hill in 1775, at the beginning of the American Revolutionary War. Much of the skirmish occurred on nearby Breed's Hill. This was a British victory over the colonial militia, but with more than 1,000 casualties. The small building at the base of the obelisk dates from the late nineteenth century and houses a statue of General Joseph Warren, a patriot who died in the battle.

HARRISON GRAY OTIS HOUSE

LOCATION: **141 Cambridge Street**

NEIGHBORHOOD: **West End**

ARCHITECT: **Charles Bulfinch**

Charles Bulfinch, architect of the U.S. Capitol and such Boston landmarks as Faneuil Hall and the Massachusetts State House, designed this Federal-style mansion in 1796 for Harrison Gray Otis, a lawyer who served in Congress and as mayor of Boston and was instrumental in developing the Beacon Hill neighborhood.

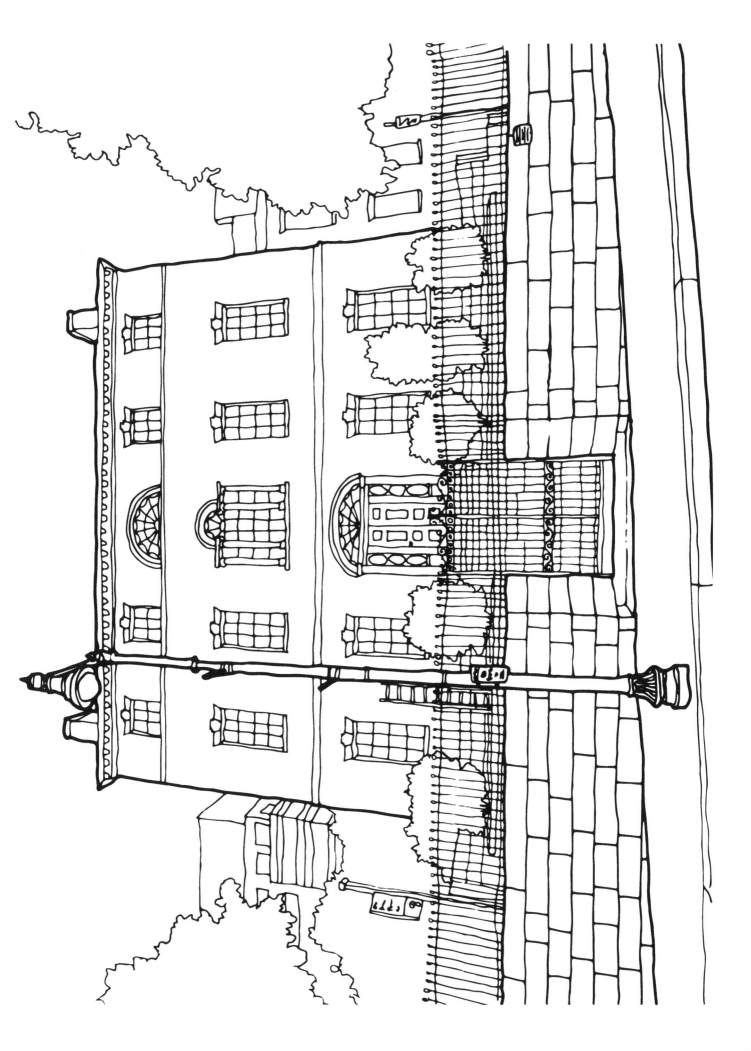

ABIEL SMITH SCHOOL, MUSEUM OF AFRICAN AMERICAN HISTORY

LOCATION: **46 Joy Street**

NEIGHBORHOOD: **Beacon Hill**

ARCHITECT: **Richard Upjohn**

This small building was constructed in 1834 as the first public school for African American children. Located in the north end of Beacon Hill, once the residential center of the black community, the building sits adjacent to the African Meeting House, where the school was previously located. The building is named for Abiel Smith, a white businessman and philanthropist who left money to the city of Boston for the education of black children. Today, it contains galleries for exhibitions, educational programs, a museum store, and a kitchen.

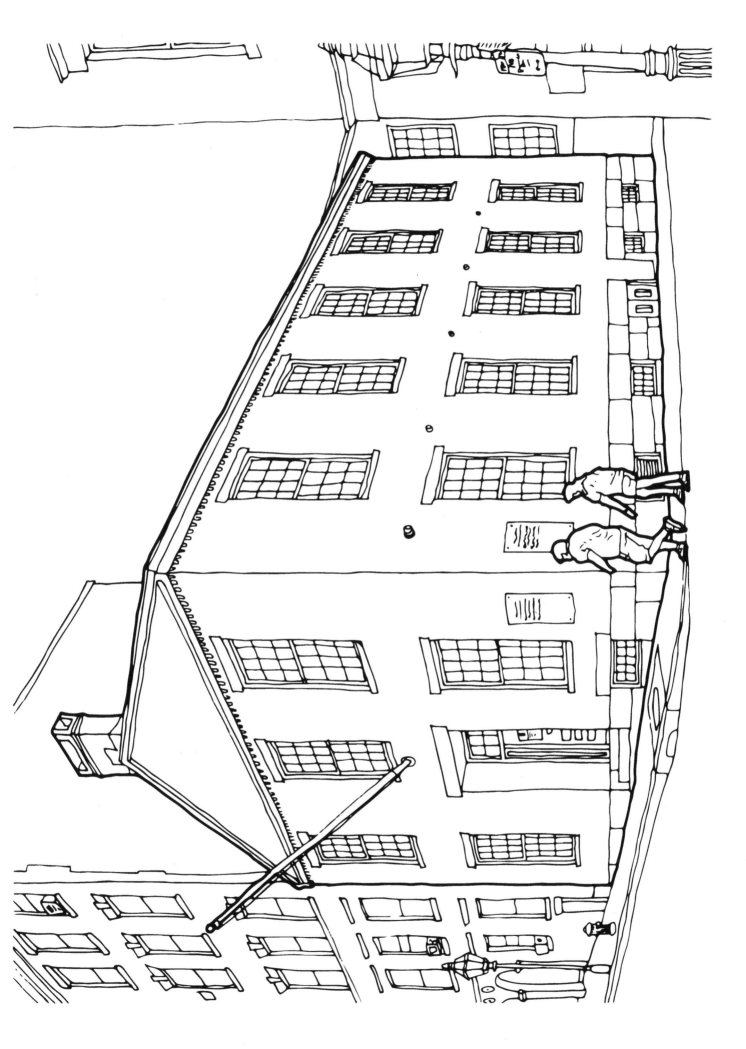

VILNA SHUL

LOCATION: **18 Phillips Street**

NEIGHBORHOOD: **Beacon Hill**

ARCHITECT: **Max Kalman**

Built primarily by immigrants from Vilna, Lithuania, as a synagogue on Beacon Hill, the building's cornerstone was laid in 1919. Once covered in beige paint, three murals adorn the interior walls, rare examples of prewar Jewish art in the United States. Remaining members held the last Rosh Hashanah service in 1985. Today, the Vilna Shul is Boston's center for Jewish culture, with a cultural center, community center, and museum.

CHEERS (HAMPSHIRE HOUSE)

LOCATION: **84 Beacon Street**

NEIGHBORHOOD: **Beacon Hill**

ARCHITECT: **Ogden Codman**

This building was built in 1910 as a five-story Georgian Revival townhouse for Bayard and Ruth Thayer. Located near Boston Public Garden, it was a popular site of the Boston social scene in its early years. During WWII, when the building was sold and turned into a luxury hotel, it became known as the Hampshire House. The basement pub was originally called the Bull & Finch Pub, established in 1969 by Thomas A. Kershaw. This pub inspired the NBC sitcom *Cheers*, which ran on air from 1982 to 1993. Today, the building is a popular destination for tourists seeking to reconnect with this celebrated sitcom.

MASSACHUSETTS STATE HOUSE

LOCATION: **24 Beacon Street**

NEIGHBORHOOD: **Beacon Hill**

ARCHITECTS: **Charles Bulfinch;
Charles Brigham (1895 annex);
Gridley Bryant (1853 addition);
Richard Sturgis (1914–17 additions)**

Completed in 1798, the Massachusetts State House overlooks Boston Common on land once owned by John Hancock. The Massachusetts Legislature meets here and the building houses offices of the governor, governor's council, and cabinet. The dome was originally made of wood and covered in copper by Paul Revere. In 1874, it was painted in 23-karat gold leaf, but it was painted gray during WWII to reduce visibility as a protective measure. The dome is topped with a gilded wooden pinecone that references the state's reliance on logging in the eighteenth century. The building is open to the public for tours.

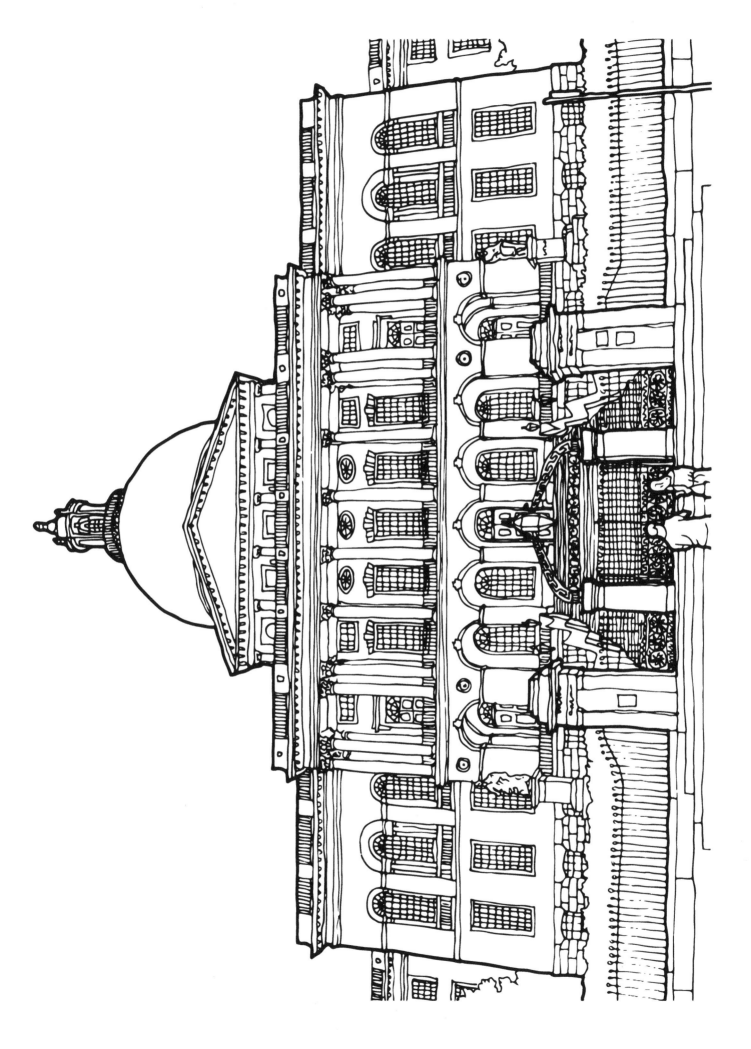

CPSIA information can be obtained
at www.ICGtesting.com
Printed in the USA
BVHW021239210819
556419BV00016B/728/P